GEORGE S. PATTON

An Outstanding General

THE HISTORY HOUR

HISTORY

CONTENTS

I
INTRODUCTION

"Lead me, follow me, or get out of my way."

— GEORGE S. PATTON

One of the greatest military heroes of modern American history was General George S. Patton. He was a colorful, high-energy soldier who met with great success on the battlefield and consternation in other areas of his public life. This troops loved him, but the Allied high command was less convinced.

What makes Patton a controversial figure, and who was he,

really? From privileged birth to Olympic athlete to conqueror, this is the story of George S. Patton.

II

BORN TO BE A SOLDIER

"Accept the challenges, so that you may feel the exhilaration of victory."

— GEORGE S. PATTON

George Smith Patton, Jr., was born in San Gabriel, California on November 11, 1885. His was the first born and only son of George Smith Patton, Sr., and his wife, Ruth Wilson. His younger sister, Anne Wilson Patton, called Nita, made his family a happy foursome.

MILITARY ROOTS RUN DEEP

Patton's family was descended from the Welsh lords of Glamorgan, men who had a long history of military service and accomplishment reaching back into the Middle Ages. His family also descended from King Edward I of England through the king's son, Edmund of Woodstock, the 1st Earl of Kent. Family fable held that he was also descended from 16 of the Scottish barons who had signed the Magna Carta, the famous document that limited royal power for the first time in human history.

The first Patton to come to North America was Robert Patton, born in Ayr, Scotland, who emigrated to Virginia in 1769 or 1770. He likely fought as a patriot in the American Revolution. During the American Civil War, Patton's grandfather, George Smith Patton, commanded the 22nd Virginia Infantry under famed commander Jubal Early. He was killed in the Third Battle of Winchester. Meanwhile, his great-uncle, Walter Patton, was killed during Pickett's Charge at the Battle of Gettysburg. On his mother's side, he descended from Hugh Mercer, a Patriot who had been killed at the Battle of Princeton during the American Revolution. George Smith Patton Sr., Patton's father, graduated from the Virginia Military Institute and went on to become the district attorney of Los Angeles, California.

Patton never had any intention to be anything other than a soldier. He was an intelligent and inquisitive boy who loved to read military history, especially books recounting the exploits of Hannibal, Scipio Africanus, Julius Caesar, Joan of Arc and Napoleon Bonaparte. Patton family friend John Singleton Mosby, a frequent guest in their house during his childhood, was also known as the "***Gray Ghost***" for his raids and ability to escape capture when he was a Confederate cavalry leader. His tales of warfare entranced young George and added to his urgent wish to be a soldier, as well.

Patton's ancestry was greatly important to him, and he claimed deep spiritual ties to the men who had come before him. He believed in reincarnation, and his deep conviction that he had been a soldier in several lifetimes became a central part of his personal identity. He pursued rigorous physical training, and he became an expert equestrian.

MILITARY ACADEMY

When he was seventeen years old, he tried to gain entrance to the United States Military Academy, and he also applied to multiple universities with Reserve Officer Training Corps programs. He was accepted to Princeton but ultimately decided to attend the Virginia Military Institute, which had been the alma mater for his father and grandfather. He was nominated to West Point by a senator from California, and so his dream was realized, and he headed to Annapolis.

His transition to military routine was smooth and untroubled, but his academics caused him some strain. In fact, his mathematics scores were so low that he was forced to repeat his first year. He improved his academic performance somewhat, but his scholarly endeavors were always overshadowed by his brilliance at military drills. He was made cadet sergeant major during his junior year and cadet adjutant during his senior year, both very prestigious positions. He played football for West Point but suffered several arm injuries. Because of his issues on the football team, Patton switched to fencing and track and field, specializing in the modern pentathlon.

OLYMPIAN

❧

In 1912, at the Olympic Games in Stockholm, Sweden, Patton competed as the Army's representative. He contended in the first modern pentathlon and finished well. On the pistol range, he finished at 21st place, but the rest of his placements were much better: 7th in swimming, 4th in fencing, 6th in the equestrian competition and 3rd in the footrace. He finished 5th overall, behind four members of the host country's delegation.

❧

His placement in the shooting competition caused some controversy. Patton was shooting with a 38 caliber pistol, while all the rest of the competitors were using 22 caliber guns. Patton maintained that the holes he made in the targets were so large that his later shots went through them without leaving a trace, but the judges ruled that he had missed completely at least one. If his argument had been accepted, he would have won the gold medal.

❦

On the way back from the Olympics, Patton traveled to Saumur, France, where he studied fencing under Adjutant Charles Cléry, an instructor and master at arms at a French cavalry academy.

FIRST COMMISSION

When he graduated from West Point, he was ranked 46th out of 103, and he was commissioned as a second lieutenant in the Cavalry Branch of the US Army. His first posting was with the 15th Cavalry at Fort Sheridan, Illinois, where he distinguished himself as an aggressive and spirited leader. His superiors were impressed, and he was transferred to Fort Myer in Virginia, where many of the Army's senior officers were stationed. He befriended Henry L. Stimson, the Secretary of War, and served as his aide at social functions. He was also the quartermaster officer for his unit.

While at Fort Myer, Patton took what he had learned from Cléry and applied it to the US Cavalry, redesigning saber combat standards, switching the emphasis from slashing attacks to thrusting. He was temporarily assigned to the

Office of the Army Chief of Staff, where he designed a new version of the cavalry saber. The design was well received, and in 1913, the first 20,000 of the Model 1913 Cavalry Saber, known as the "***Patton sword***," were ordered.

❧

With his new weapon in hand, Patton returned to Saumur for more study under Cléry, where he learned advanced techniques that he brought back with him to the Mounted Service School at Fort Riley, Kansas. He was both a student and an instructor, and he became the first American cavalry officer to be declared "***Master of the Sword***."

❧

In 1913, Patton was assigned to the 15th Cavalry, which was about to be deployed in the Philippines. He was convinced that this assignment would dead-end his career, so he prevailed upon influential friends in Washington, D.C., to have him reassigned. He successfully lobbied for and received an assignment to the 8th Cavalry at Fort Bliss, Texas, which was on high alert due to unrest in neighboring Mexico.

❧

In 1916, he was selected to return to the Olympics, but the Games were canceled due to World War I.

III
FOREIGN WARS

"The object of war is not to die for your country but to make the other bastard die for his."

— GEORGE S. PATTON

The next decade saw Patton becoming embroiled in two very different military campaigns, both of which would shape his behavior and his fighting style in years to come.

PANCHO VILLA

❦

Mexico was in the grips of civil war when Patton arrived in Texas. There were two contenders for the control of the country: Pancho Villa and his Villistas, who were largely drawn from the native Mexicans and poor farmers, and Venustiano Carranza, whose Carrancitas were made up of the mostly Spanish-born landed elite. There had been vicious fighting, with many casualties, including among civilians.

❦

In 1915, the United States recognized Carranza as the head of the Mexican government, and they provided rail transportation from Eagle Pass, Texas, to Douglas, Arizona, for more than 5,000 Carrancitas to battle Villa at the Battle of Agua Prieta, where Villa's northern division was decimated.

❦

In retaliation, and feeling betrayed by the Americans, Villa sent raiders against American civilians and their property in northern Mexico. On November 26, 1915, Villa led his soldiers to attack the city of Nogales, where he engaged with American armed forces before he retreated across the border.

The raid on Nogales was only the beginning. On January 11, 1916, Villa seized sixteen American employees of the American Smelting and Refining Company at Santa Isabel, California. He took the men from a train and had them stripped and executed.

News of this outrage reached General John J. Pershing, the army commander at Fort Bliss, Texas, where Patton was serving. The intelligence received indicated that Villa was about to launch an attack on the United States that would force the American military to intervene, which would have been a terrible embarrassment to the Carranza government. Villa was not seen as a credible threat, however, and the intel was dismissed.

On March 9, 1916, Villa crossed the border and attacked Columbus, New Mexico, and the American army base at Camp Furlong. The troop detail at Camp Furlong consisted of four troops of the 13th Cavalry, about 240 men who had been stationed there since 1912. It was a daring attack for Villa to make, and in the aftermath, it was found that ten civilians and eight soldiers had been killed. Two civilians and six soldiers had been wounded. The Villistas had also burned the town, stolen horses and mules, seized machine guns and ammunition from the fort, and stole merchandise from the town's shops before crossing back into Mexico.

❧

The Villistas, though they inflicted damage, were badly injured themselves. They left 67 dead behind them, and there were dozens of wounded men. Most of the injuries came at the hands of the machine gun crew of the 13th Cavalry in defense of Camp Furlong, who had fired over 5,000 rounds in the fight. Five of the Villistas were arrested and hanged for murder. Local legend holds that the reason for the raid was that a storekeeper in Columbus had been supplying Villa with arms and ammunition, but inexplicably decided to take Villa's cash and refused to provide him with the goods unless Villa could pay in gold. The raid was retaliation for this insult.

❧

US President Woodrow Wilson ordered General Frederick Funston, the commander of the southern department of the cavalry, to form an expedition force to pursue and stop Pancho Villa. When the plans for the expedition reached Fort Bliss, Patton realized that his unit was not to be included. He immediately went to his superior, General John J. Pershing, and pushed to be part of the Pancho Villa Expedition. Patton was named Pershing's personal aide for the duration of the action. He took a hand in planning the invasion of Mexico, and his enthusiasm and dedication impressed Pershing, whose own command style was exemplified by strong, decisive action. Patton based his own leadership style on Pershing's, and it would serve him well in the future. Patton acted as Pershing's personal courier, carrying the general's orders to senior staff.

❧

In mid-April 1916, Pershing rewarded Patton with command of Troop C of the 13th Cavalry, tasked with assisting in the manhunt for Villa and his associates. He had his first taste of combat on May 14, 1916, a date that also featured the first use of motorized combat in American military history. On that day, Patton's command of ten soldiers and two civilian guides with the 6th Infantry, riding in three Dodge touring cars, happened upon three Villistas, catching them in the midst of a foraging expedition. In the ensuing firefight, Patton shot all three Villistas, who later died of their injuries. This exploit gained Patton the approval of General Pershing as well as attention in the media, who labeled him "***the bandit killer***." He was promoted to the first lieutenant shortly thereafter.

❧

At the end of 1916, President Woodrow Wilson issued an order that the American forces were not to pursue any aggressive action in Mexican territory. Patton and his unit remained on the border, where they occupied themselves with training.

❧

The expedition officially ended in February 1917.

WORLD WAR I

❧

When the United States entered the fighting in World War I, the American Expeditionary Force (AEF) was put under Pershing's command and deployed to the Western Front. Patton asked to join Pershing's staff, and the request was granted. He was promoted to captain on May 15, 1917 and left for Europe with Pershing's advance party of 180 men. He began to work as Pershing's personal aide, and as such he oversaw the training received by the American troops in Paris.

❧

Patton stayed in Paris until September, when he was reassigned to Chaumont as post adjutant. He was responsible for commanding the headquarters company that ran the base. He disliked the assignment and again asked Pershing for a more active role. He was fascinated by tanks, which had appeared on the battlefield for the first time. Pershing again complied with Patton's requests, this time assigning him the command of an infantry battalion.

❧

Patton developed jaundice at this time, and he was hospitalized in France. While he was there, he met Colonel Fox Conner, an operations officer with the AEF. Conner encouraged Patton to work with tanks instead of the infantry, and another request was sent off to General Pershing.

❧

On November 10, 1917, Patton was put in charge of creating the AEF Light Tank School. In preparation for this job, he went to Champlieu to work with the French tank corps at their training school. While at Champlieu, he learned to drive a tank, specifically the Renault FT light tank, which impressed him greatly. He was determined that the United States Army should have tanks, as well.

❧

The British launched an assault on Cambrai using more tanks in one action than any force had ever used before. Patton traveled to Albert, which was 30 miles from Cambrai, to discuss the performance of the tanks with Colonel J. F. C. Fuller, who was the chief of staff of the British Tank Corps. He was encouraged by what he heard, and he became even more dedicated to adding tanks to the army's repertoire. He returned to Paris and the AEF, stopping along the way at the Renault factory to watch tanks being manufactured. Patton was promoted to major on January 26, 1918.

❧

In March, Patton received ten tanks from the Renault factory, which were delivered to the Tank School at Bourg. Patton was the only US soldier who knew how to drive a tank, so he personally drove seven of the tanks off of the train that delivered them. He worked to train tank crews and tried to persuade infantry commanders to add tanks to their battle plans. The infantry commanders were reticent to include tanks, which up until then had been notorious for breaking down and were considered essentially novelty items that wouldn't last. Patton was persuasive. Tanks were added to the AEF's plans.

❧

He was promoted again in April 1918, this time to Lieutenant Colonel, and with his new rank came more training at the Command and General Staff College at Langres. He was given the command of the US 1st Provisional Tank Brigade in August 1918, attached to the American First Army as part of Colonel Samuel Rockenbach's Tank Corps. Patton was intent upon proving the tanks' worth in combat, and he oversaw all of the logistics of the action. This was to be the first time the American military used tanks, and he wanted nothing to go wrong. He personally scouted the target area for the first attack, and he issued an order that no American tank was to be surrendered for any reason.

❧

The first use of tanks by the American army came at the Battle of Saint-Mihiel, a major offensive combining American and French forces in an assault against German positions.

The battle took place over three days, September 12, 1918, through September 15, 1918. Patton led his tank corps from the front, even walking in front of the tanks going into the village of Essey, which was in German hands, and once riding on top of a tank during the assault on the town of Pannes. He was an inspiration to his troops.

❧

On September 26, 1918, Patton and his tanks were reassigned to support the U. S. I Corps in the Meuse-Argonne Offensive, the largest engagement in the war involving US forces. Patton personally led a detachment of tanks through thick fog as they advanced on German lines. He was leading six men and a tank in an attack on a German machine gun nest when he was shot in the left leg. He was pulled from the battlefield by his orderly, Private First-Class Joe Angelo, who saved his life and was awarded the Distinguished Service Cross for his bravery. Patton commanded the attack from the safety of a shell hole for over an hour before he was evacuated. He insisted on submitting his report to the rear command post before he would go to the field hospital. He was proud of the way his tanks had performed, and he wanted everyone to know it.

❧

Patton's wound was serious. He described it in a letter to his wife in this way:

> *"The bullet went into the front of my left leg and came out just at the crack of my bottom about two inches to the left of my rectum. It was fired at*

about 50 m so made a hole about the size of a dollar where it came out."

This deeply unpleasant injury kept him out of the fighting until the war ended on November 11, 1918, although he returned to duty on October 28, 1918, with the new rank of colonel.

❧

For his wartime service, Patton received the Distinguished Service Cross, the Distinguished Service Medal, and (when the award was created in 1932) a Purple Heart.

IV
BETWEEN THE WARS

"Better to fight for something than live for nothing."

— GEORGE S. PATTON

Between the two world wars, Patton continued to serve in the army. His battlefield promotions were rolled back when he returned from France, and he was reassigned to Camp Meade in Maryland at the rank of captain. He was promoted to major the very next day.

TANK CHAMPION

When Patton returned to the United States, he was convinced that tanks should be independent of the infantry as their own unit rather than acting in a supportive capacity. Shortly after his assignment to Camp Meade, he was sent to Washington, D.C., where he served on a committee dedicated to writing a manual on tank operations. At this time he supported a new tank design, the M1919, which was ultimately not produced because of budgetary concerns.

While he was in Washington, Patton met and befriended Dwight D. Eisenhower. He and Eisenhower began to correspond, and Patton even sent notes that helped his friend to graduate from General Staff College. Along with Eisenhower and J. Walter Christie, the designer of the M1919 tank, Patton pushed for development of armored divisions. Secretary of War Dwight Davis agreed with them, but the money simply wasn't there due to the expense of the war that had just been fought. An armored corps would not be developed until just before the Second World War.

❧

On September 30, 1920, Patton was given command of the 3rd Squadron, 3rd Cavalry at Fort Myer. He hated it. Peacetime didn't suit him and working as a staff officer when there was no action made him restless. He contented himself with writing technical papers and giving speeches at the General Staff College about his wartime experiences. He joined the American Legion Tank Corps Post No.19 in July 1921, and from 1922 to the middle of 1923 he attended the Field Officer's Course at the Cavalry School at Fort Riley. He then went to the Command and General Staff College until mid-1924, where he graduated 25th in a class of 248.

❧

In August 1923, Patton saved the lives of several children when they fell from a yacht during a boating excursion off the coast from Salem, Massachusetts. He received the Silver Lifesaving Medal for this rescue.

❧

He was briefly stationed in Boston with the General Staff Corps, but in March 1925 he was reassigned as G-1 and later G-2 of the Hawaiian Division at Schofield Barracks in Honolulu, Hawaii.

❧

Patton served as G-3 of the Hawaiian Division for several months, but then he was transferred back to Washington, D.C., in May 1927. He was attached to the Office of the Chief of Cavalry, and while he was there, he began to work on developing and expanding the understanding and use of mechanized warfare. His work resulted in a brief attempt to merge infantry, cavalry, and artillery into a combined unit, but Congress voted to remove funding from the project, and it was canceled. Still feeling dissatisfied, Patton left the office in 1931 to enroll in the Army War College, leaving as a "***Distinguished Graduate***" in 1932.

THE BONUS ARMY

❧

In the summer of 1932, over 43,000 people, including over 17,000 World War I veterans and their families, converged on Washington, D.C. in protest over the bonuses they had received for their wartime service. These bonuses were paid in the form of certificates, but when they tried to exchange the certificates for cash, they were advised that they could not redeem them until 1945. This was during the height of the Great Depression, and many of these veterans were without work. They came to demand that the government redeem the certificates immediately for cash.

❧

On July 28, 1932, U.S. Attorney General William D. Mitchell issued an order telling the civil authorities to remove the veterans from government property, including the area where they had built shelters for their families for the duration of the protest. When police from Washington, D.C., tried to clear the crowd, an armed brawl broke out during which shots were fired. Two of the veterans were killed.

❧

President Herbert Hoover turned to the Army. Patton's 600-man 3rd Cavalry was ordered by Army Chief of Staff General Douglas MacArthur to disperse the protesters. Patton was displeased by the orders, because he had sympathy with the veterans' cause, and because he himself had earlier refused to issue an order to use force in removing the protesters. He nevertheless led a force of infantry and cavalry with six tanks down Pennsylvania Avenue to force the veterans to leave. The protesters and their families were driven away from their makeshift camp, and their belongings and tents were destroyed. Patton found this duty "***most distasteful***," but he believed that it was necessary to prevent property destruction and further loss of life.

HAWAII

Patton received another promotion on March 1, 1934, this time to lieutenant colonel. He was transferred once again to the Hawaiian Division and returned to Honolulu.

While in Hawaii, Patton became a student of the aggression of the Japanese Empire. He watched in alarm as the Japanese military committed atrocities against Chinese civilians during the Sino-Japanese War that began in 1937. Based on his observations, he formulated a plan to intern Japanese people living in Hawaii in the event of a Japanese surprise attack, which he predicted in his paper "***Surprise***."

Contrary to many people in civilian life, Patton hoped for an armed conflict, and when none materialized while he was in Hawaii, he developed a problem with drink. He also began an extramarital affair with Jean Gordon, who was his 21-year-old niece by marriage. At the time, he was 49. His infidelity nearly destroyed his marriage, but he was able to convince his wife to stay with him by expressing remorse for his actions, one of the few times in his life that he would do so.

❧

He returned to Los Angeles for an extended leave in 1937, and while he was playing polo, he suffered a broken leg after being kicked by a horse. He then developed phlebitis, which was nearly fatal. He was nearly forced out of active duty because of the phlebitis and his injury, but a recovered thanks to a six-month administrative assignment at the Academic Department at the Cavalry School at Fort Riley.

❧

He was promoted to colonel on July 24, 1938 and took command of the 5th Cavalry at Fort Clark in Texas. He served there for six months before he was reassigned to Fort Myer as commander of the 3rd Cavalry. It was at Fort Myer that he met Army Chief of Staff George C. Marshall, who considered Patton an excellent candidate for promotion to the rank of general.

❧

Patton was bored with peacetime. Luckily for him, unluckily for the world, his boredom was about to end.

V
WORLD WAR II BEGINS

"Never tell people how to do things. Tell them what to do and they will surprise you with their ingenuity."

— GEORGE S. PATTON

In September 1939, Adolf Hitler's Nazi Germany invaded Poland, and the Second World War began. The United States began to mobilize, and Patton became involved in the build-up of the armored corps.

In 1940, the Third Army conducted maneuvers where Patton served as an umpire. While he was involved in this exercise, he met Adna R. Chaffee, Jr., who shared Patton's passion for tanks and mechanized warfare. Chaffee and Patton put together recommendations for the development of an armored corps.

❧

The 1st and 2nd Armored Divisions were created, and Chaffee was the commander. Patton was appointed the commander of the 2nd Armored Brigade, which was part of the 2nd Armored Division, and put in charge of its training. The 2nd Armored Division was formulated from the start as a heavy formation, and it had many tanks in its control, one of the few to be contemplated as a truly armored unit from the outset.

❧

Patton was again promoted, this time to brigadier general, and made acting division commander. In 1941, he was promoted again, this time to major general. He was appointed Commanding General (CG) of the 2nd Armored Division, and after Chaffee stepped down from his command of the I Armored Corps, Patton became the number one man in the United States Army's armored service.

PRACTICE MAKES PERFECT

In December 1940, Patton staged a practice exercise in which 1,000 tanks and armored vehicles traveled from Columbus, Georgia to Panama City, Florida, and back. The training maneuver attracted a great deal of attention, and Patton and his tanks began to gain notoriety.

In January 1941, he led his men on another high-profile exercise, this time involving 1,300 vehicles and tanks. Patton earned a pilot's license, so he could watch the maneuver from the air, which he hoped would help him learn new ways to deploy tanks in combat. Due to these endeavors, he ended up on the cover of Life magazine.

In June 1941, he led his division through the Tennessee

Maneuvers, in nine hours successfully completing mission objectives that were planned to take two days. In September, during the Louisiana Maneuvers, he was part of the Red Army (not to be confused with Soviet forces, who were not involved in the exercise). His group lost in Phase I, but during Phase II, he was assigned to the Blue Army, which executed an end run around the Red Army, which covered 400 miles and led to the successful "***capture***" of Shreveport, Louisiana. More training exploits were to come. In October and November 1941, Patton's unit captured the commanding officer of their "***enemy***," Hugh Drum, who had been the first United States Army Chief of Staff during World War I.

He was tasked with establishing the Desert Training Center in the Imperial Valley of California, where he began to run training exercises in late 1941, continuing into the next year. The Desert Training Center occupied a 10,000-acre patch of desert southeast of Palm Springs.

On January 15, 1942, after the United States had entered the war, Patton was placed in command of I Armored Corps, who started drilling at the Desert Training Center. From the beginning, Patton emphasized a need to keep in constant contact with the enemy, with a marked preference for offensive actions as opposed to defensive strategies. He believed in speed and aggression, something that typified his command style and his military career as a whole.

NORTH AFRICAN CAMPAIGN

Lieutenant Dwight D. Eisenhower, Patton's friend, had been named Supreme Allied Commander, and he assigned Patton to help plan the Allied invasion of French North Africa that would come to be called Operation Torch. Patton was to be in command of the Western Task Force, which would consist of 33,000 men who landed in Morocco in November 1942.

The Vichy French army input up against a bloody-minded defense, but despite this opposition, Patton's men were able to establish a beachhead and force their way inland. They took Casablanca on November 11, and Patton negotiated the terms of the Vichy French surrender with General Charles Nogués. Upon the conquest of Casablanca, the Sultan of Morocco presented him with the Order of Ouissam Alaouite, along with a citation translating to

"The lions in their dens tremble at his approach."

Under Patton's direction, Morocco was converted into a military port, and in January 1943, he hosted the Casablanca Conference, a strategy meeting attended by US President Franklin D. Roosevelt and British Prime Minister Winston Churchill.

❧

The US II Corps was defeated by the German Afrika Korps under General Erwin Rommel at the Battle of Kasserine Pass in February 1943. The battle took place in a two-mile-wide gap in the Grand Dorsai Mountains, part of the Atlas Mountains in Tunisia. In this, the first major clash of American and German forces in World War II's African Theater, the Americans were poorly led and inexperienced. They suffered massive casualties and were pushed back 50 miles from their original positions. It was a disaster.

❧

Patton responded by changing the commanders of the unit. Major General Lloyd Fredenall was made Commanding General of the II Corps and was promoted to lieutenant general. The deputy commander was Major General Omar Bradley. In an effort to shake up the demoralized men, Patton instituted a number of changes that were designed to improve them as soldiers. They were ordered to adhere to military discipline and protocol in all things, including the requirement that they wear clean, ironed and complete uniforms at all times. They were also given rigorous schedules and duties. Patton pushed them hard, but he also rewarded success.

❧

Patton expected all of his soldiers, whether officers or enlisted, to be fully dedicated and engaged to the fight. He would not accept anything less. He ordered an attack on a hill near Gafsa, and the orders that were sent to the units involved included the following:

> *"I expect to see such casualties among officers, particularly staff officers, as will convince me that a serious effort has been made to capture this objective."*

Nobody got an easy ride when Patton was around.

❧

On March 17, 1942, after enduring Patton's reforms and training, the US 1st Infantry Division took that hill and the rest of Gafsa, winning the Battle of El Guettar. In the process, they pushed back a combined force of German and Italian troops not once, but two times.

❧

The 1st Armored Division entered into conflict with a smaller German force but failed to take the day. Patton removed its commander, Major General Orlando Ward. He had taken War to task for not showing sufficient levels of personal leadership, and he considered Ward to be a tentative and overcautious leader. He was replaced by Major General Ernest N. Harmon, who had distinguished himself during the Battle of Kasserine Pass. Ward became the only general to be relieved of his command by Patton for the duration of the war.

❧

Patton extended his unforgiving attitude to his allies, as well. He complained that Air Vice Marshal Sir Arthur Coningham and his Royal Air Force were not providing American troops with sufficient close air support. Coningham and Patton both reported to the same commander, British General Sir Harold Alexander of the 18th Army Group, who assured Patton that Coningham's forces were doing everything they could. Patton remained unconvinced.

❧

Coningham sent three officers to Patton's headquarters to convince him that the air support he was receiving was more than sufficient for his needs. During the meeting, the camp was attacked by the German Luftwaffe, and part of the ceiling of Patton's office collapsed. Needless to say, air support was stepped up after this eventful discussion. Patton would later say,

> *"If I could find the sons of bitches who flew those planes, I'd mail each of them a medal."*

❧

Patton's forces pushed through to the city of Gabés, which the Germans abandoned in the face of the Allied advance. With this victory in hand, he handed the reins of II Corps to General Omar Bradley and returned to Casablanca, where he began to help plan Operation Husky.

VI
HARD FIGHTING AHEAD

"Success is how high you bounce when you hit bottom."

— GEORGE S. PATTON

Operation Husky was the codename for the Allied invasion of Sicily, which they meant to take back from the Axis Powers. The campaign would involve airborne, amphibious and land-based forces in one of the major campaigns of the war.

The goals set out for Operation Husky were ambitious. First, they were to defeat Axis air, land and naval forces and expel them from the island. Second, they were to open Allied merchant shipping lanes that had been closed since 1941. If properly performed, the operation could open the way for the Allies to invade Italy.

TAKING SICILY

Operation Husky was scheduled to begin with a simultaneous amphibious landing by two Allied armies, one on the south-eastern beaches of the island and the other on the central southern coast. In order to make these landings successful, there would be naval bombardment, tactical bombing from the air, and close air support. The combination of these forces required delicate handling and a complex command structure.

The land forces were drawn from the armies of Britain, Canada, and the United States, and they were divided into two task forces. The Eastern Task Force, which was also called Task Force 545, was under the command of General Sir Bernard Montgomery. It included the British Eighth Army and the 1st Canadian Infantry Division. The Western Task Force, also known as Task Force 343, was under Patton's command, and it consisted entirely of the American Seventh Army. Patton and Montgomery reported to British General Sir Harold Alexander, who was second-in-command to the Supreme Commander, General Eisenhower.

❧

The transport of these troops to Sicily required two additional task forces to accomplish the job. The Eastern Naval Task Force was made up of the British Mediterranean Fleet under the command of Admiral Bertram Ramsay. The Western Naval Task Force was made up of the American Eighth Fleet, led by Admiral Henry Kent Hewitt. Air support was to come from the Mediterranean Air Command (MAC), led by Air Chief Marshal Sir Arthur Tedder, whose major subcommand, the Northwest African Air Forces (NAAF) had received a detachment of medium bombers and fighter aircraft from the US Army Air Force's 9th Air Force.

❧

Before the invasion, Patton reorganized the Seventh Army into two corps and created a Provisional Corps Headquarters, which he placed under the command of Major General Geoffrey Keyes.

❧

It was a massive undertaking. The complicated interplay of military forces had been planned at the Casablanca Conference that Patton had hosted in January 1943. At the time of the meeting, all three of the mainland commanders (Alexander, Montgomery, and Patton himself) were out in the field fighting in the Tunisian campaign and could not assist with the high-level planning. That meant that some of the finer details would be decided on the ground.

❧

Patton's forces landed before dawn on the beaches near the village of Licata. There were three infantry units involved, and by the end of the first day, they had all secured their beachheads, making possible future landings by additional troops. There were counterattacks at Gela, another of the landing sites, with bombardment by German and Italian planes. The United States Navy helped the army to hold the beachhead as the Army units surged inland to take the Ponte Olivo Airfield. German reinforcements from the Herman Göring Division attempted to lend their support, but they were repulsed by the American troops, which Patton led personally.

❧

Patton's orders initially had been to protect the British forces' left flank, but when British commander Montgomery got bogged down on the road to Messina, Patton got permission to push on and take Palermo. The 3rd Infantry Division commanded by Major General Lucian Truscott, who was part of Keyes' provisional corps, raced 100 miles in 72 hours, reaching and taking Palermo on July 21, 1943. With that prize in hand, Patton turned his attention to Messina.

❧

Patton requested an amphibious assault, but due to a lack of landing craft, he had to delay until August 8th. By that time, the Germans and Italians had already evacuated many of their troops and redeployed them to mainland Italy. There were still German soldiers waiting, though, and when Patton ordered the 3rd Infantry Division to land, they were greeted with a hail of gunfire. They took heavy casualties but still managed to push the Germans back. The third landing on August 16th was the nail in the coffin, and by midnight that night, Messina had fallen.

It was a massive victory. Patton's Seventh Army had been 200,000 strong at the outset of the operation, and they lost 7,500 to injury and death. In return, however, they killed or captured 113,000 Axis soldiers and destroyed some 3,500 vehicles.

CONTROVERSY

The Sicily campaign was the first time that Patton's aggressive personal style resulted in controversies and accusations of misbehavior.

During the attack on Messina, British General Alexander had sent orders via radio that were meant to limit Patton's actions. Patton's chief of staff, Brigadier General Hobart R. Gay, claimed that these orders were "***lost in transmission***," and then he didn't receive them to convey to Patton until after Messina had fallen. The timing was suspect, to say the least.

On July 22, 1943, Patton and his armored column were blocked by a mule-drawn cart that had stopped across a bridge. Patton pulled out his signature pearl-handled pistol and shot both mules. When the owner protested, Patton proceeded to beat him with a walking stick, then dumped the dead animals into the river below.

❧

On July 14, 1943, a contingent of soldiers from the US 180th Infantry Regiment killed 73 unarmed German and Italian prisoners of war at Biscari Airfield in Santo Pietro, Sicily. When Patton learned of the atrocity, he wrote in his diary:

> *"I told Bradley that is was probably an exaggeration, but in any case, to tell the officer to certify that the dead men were snipers or had attempted to escape or something, as it would make a stink in the press and also would make the civilians mad. Anyhow, they are dead, so nothing can be done about it."*

Bradley refused Patton's suggestion, and when the 45th Division's Inspector General ruled that there had been no provocation by the prisoners and that their deaths had been pure murder, Patton changed his tune. He reportedly responded to this judgment by saying,

"Try the bastards."

SLAPPING

The most high-profile incidents that were to dog Patton for the remainder of his career involved episodes in which he struck subordinates.

On August 3, 1943, Patton met Private Charles H. Kuhl at a hospital in Nicosia. Kuhl was scheduled to be evacuated with the rest of the wounded after having been diagnosed with "***battle fatigue***," which was the term then used for PTSD (post-traumatic distress syndrome). When he learned of the diagnosis, Patton slapped and verbally abused Kuhl, calling him a coward. A similar incident took place on August 10, when the same circumstances occurred. This time Patton's victim was Private Paul G. Bennett. Patton ordered both soldiers to return to the front lines, and he issued orders for his officers to discipline any other man coming forward to seek treatment for battle fatigue.

Eisenhower was told of these incidents, and he reprimanded Patton in private. He ordered him to apologize to the men, and Patton, to his credit, apologized to both men individually as well as to the doctors and nurses who had witnessed the episode. He later apologized to all of his soldiers in several speeches.

The news of these slapping incidents was suppressed in the media through the efforts of Eisenhower, but it came to light in November on a radio program by journalist Drew Pearson. Patton was strongly criticized in the United States, and his critics included members of Congress and military veterans, including General Pershing. The general public's response was more nuanced, and Patton was retained as a commander by order of Secretary of War Henry L. Stimson, who said that Patton's aggressive nature was needed at the front.

For eleven months, Patton did not command any forces in the field. In September 1943, General Omar Bradley, who was Patton's subordinate, was put in charge of the First United States Army, which was forming in England in preparation for Operation Overlord. Patton believed that he was passed over for this command because of the slapping incidents, even though the decision to place Bradley in that position had been taken long before.

The truth was that the slapping incidents confirmed the decision to promote Bradley. Eisenhower felt that the act of slapping those two soldiers displayed Patton's inability to exercise personal discipline, as well as a certain lack of self-control. The landing in Europe for D-Day was considered too important to leave anything to chance, and it was thought that Bradley would be less impulsive and less given to making rash decisions.

❧

As a sort of consolation prize, Patton was put in command of the US Third Army, which was then being created in England. His orders were to train the men and get them ready for combat in Europe, and he fulfilled those orders for the first half of 1944.

VII
NORMANDY

"May God have mercy upon my enemies, because I won't."

— GEORGE S. PATTON

At the Trident Conference in Washington, D.C., in May 1943, the northwestern coast of France in the region of Normandy was selected as the site of the Allied invasion of Europe. The specific beaches were codenamed and assigned: Utah and Omaha to the Americans, Sword and Gold to the British, and Juno to the forces from Canada. Secrecy about the battle plans was absolute, and the Germans were misled about the location and timing of the attack through a large-scale exercise of military deception called Operation Bodyguard. Patton would have a pivotal part to play.

OPERATION FORTITUDE

❧

Out of all of the Allied commanders, Patton was the one that the German High Command respected the most. They believed that any invasion of Europe would necessarily include his involvement. Because of this interest from the enemy, Operation Fortitude was designed around him.

❧

Operation Fortitude was meant to mislead the Germans regarding the location of the invasion when it ultimately took place. The operation was so massive that it was divided into two sub-plans, North and South. Both of these plans surrounded the creation of phantom field armies that were "***threatening***" Norway (Fortitude North) and Pas de Calais in France (Fortitude South). The intent was to deflect the attention of the Axis powers away from Normandy and to convince them that the Normandy invasion was only a diversionary tactic.

❧

The planning of the operation fell to the London Controlling Section (LCS), which was a secret unit dedicated to deception strategy. The actual execution, however, depended upon the commanders in the field and their understanding and willingness to cooperate. The commanders were directed by the Supreme Headquarters Allied Expeditionary Force (SHAEF), which was under General Eisenhower. A special unit was created within SHAEF called Ops (B), which was to manage the operation on the battlefield. Meanwhile, the LCS would control and direct the "***special means***" in the plan – diplomatic channels and double agents.

❧

The double agents of LCS's "***special means***" fed a stream of false information to German Intelligence by way of a network of double agents. These reports largely centered on Patton's person and activities. Through the work of these spies, the Germans were informed that Patton had been appointed to command the First United States Army Group (FUSAG) and that he would be leading a massive invasion at Calais. Meanwhile, British general Montgomery would be commanding the smaller 21st Army Group further south. This "***21st Army Group***" was the actual Normandy invasion force.

❧

The deception was not as straightforward as handing the

Germans false battle plans. Instead, there were hints and inferences given that would be misconstrued and would lead them to determine a false order of battle. The actual invasion force was building up in England, and the Germans were well aware of these troop movements. Army units and parts of the Allied invasion force would be staged around probable points of embarkation, and FUSAG was heavily concentrated in the south-east, across from Calais. The Germans deduced that the mass of the invasion force was centered here, with Patton at the helm.

FUSAG didn't even exist. It was made up of props and buildings, dummy airplanes and fake landing craft. There were multiple decoys, and fake radio signal traffic in and around Dover was meant to be overheard by German spy planes. The chatter indicated that a large force was being built up there under Patton's command, and Patton himself got involved by being photographed while visiting these fake locations, making the Germans believe that he was in Dover preparing for invasion. Meanwhile, Patton himself was still with the Third Army, overseeing their training. He was ordered to keep a low profile so that the deception that he was in Dover could be maintained.

The Operation was a huge success. The German 15th Army stayed in Calais to defend against an invasion that never came, and even after D-Day and the Allied invasion through Normandy, this field army held its position, waiting for Patton.

❦

Meanwhile, Patton flew to France in July 1944 to resume his field command.

THE NORMANDY OFFENSIVE

❧

Patton and his Third Army went to France in July 1944, where they took up position on the extreme right flank of the Allied forces, under Bradley's Twelfth United States Army Group. Their orders were to attack west into Brittany, then to turn south and east toward the Seine, the river that runs through Paris. They were then to turn back northward, forming a sort of net between Falaise and Argentan that came to be called the Falaise Pocket.

❧

The attack strategy that Patton formulated was based on speed and aggressive offensive action. The Third Army utilized advance scouts to report back on enemy concentrations and positions. The "***spearhead***" units were accompanied by self-propelled artillery, which were kept to the front of the line, ready to be called into action at a moment's notice. Patton also got help from the air, with light aircraft performing reconnaissance and acting as artillery spotters.

❧

Under Patton, the infantry would lead the first charge, supported by tanks. More armored units would come up from the rear and break through the enemy lines, taking advantage of any breaches and constantly attacking, pushing the Germans back before they could regroup and counterattack. The tanks would advance using reconnaissance by fire, which is when artillery and other units fire on likely, but not confirmed, enemy positions in the hope of triggering a reaction. When the enemy troops ran to get out of the way of these test bombs, they revealed their positions and made it easier for them to be eliminated. Using this technique, Patton's Third Army found and eliminated many German ambushes.

❧

Patton and his men moved with lightning speed. They covered 60 miles in just two weeks, pushing the German forces back. They coordinated with Ultra intelligence, using information obtained at Bletchley Park in England by special code breakers who decrypted enemy transmissions. This information helped him know where the Germans were preparing to counterattack, and with this knowledge, he could concentrate his forces in the areas where they would do the most good.

LORRAINE CAMPAIGN

Patton's advance ground to a halt on August 31, 1944, when his Third Army literally ran out of gas. They reached the Moselle River, near the fortress of Metz, before they had to stop. Patton had believed that Eisenhower would have kept fuel and supplies available to support his rapid advance, but the Supreme Commander worried that Patton was getting too far ahead, so he diverted supplies to Operation Market Garden in Holland.

Patton was livid and frustrated. He believed that he was close enough to Germany that he could be on enemy soil within two days. Instead, he had to stop, watch and wait as the German Panzers prepared and launched a counterattack. The Panzers were beaten back by the US 4th Armored Division in the Battle of Arracourt. Even though the reason for the Third Army's halt was lack of resources, and despite the fact that they lost the battle, the German Panzer commanders believed that they had successfully stopped Patton's advance.

❧

The halt of Patton's advance was a boon for the Germans, who were given time to fortify their position at Metz. The Third Army and the Germans became embroiled in a two-month stalemate called the Battle of Metz in November and December of 1944, with both sides losing many men. Patton attempted to take Fort Driant, another fortification just south of Metz, but he was repulsed.

❧

It was during this time that Patton gave a press conference, during which a reporter took him to task for moving too quickly with the Third Army. Patton's response was,

> *"Whenever you slow anything down, you waste human lives."*

Another reporter paraphrased something Patton said in a speech – that it took "***blood and brains***" to win in combat – and started calling him "***Blood and Guts***." He carried that nickname for the rest of his life.

❧

Metz finally fell to the Americans in November 1944. His decisions during this campaign were roundly criticized. Even a captured German officer expressed astonishment that Patton had spent so much time on the capture of Metz when he could easily have gone around it and cut off the German

Fifth Army in Luxembourg. Captured German commander General Hermann Black stated that Patton's methods of taking the fortress were too circuitous and that a more straightforward attack would have enjoyed more success. For once, Patton was being criticized for not being aggressive enough.

❧

Even though he had taken the fortress, his supplies were still coming in at a trickle. He was forced to crawl, and between November 8 and December 15, the Third Army only advanced a total of 40 miles.

VIII
THE BATTLE OF THE BULGE

"If everyone is thinking alike, then someone isn't thinking."

— GEORGE S. PATTON

In December 1944, German Field Marshal Gerd von Rundstedt gathered up every able-bodied boy and old man in Germany and launched a desperate, last-ditch campaign through Belgium, Luxembourg, and France. He assembled 29 divisions, a force of 250,000 men, and exploited a weak spot in the Allied lines with an all-out attack on December 16, 1944. They gained ground, moving toward the Meuse River. As if to compound the misery of the German offensive, Europe entered into the coldest winter it had seen in years.

The weather was as much of a force to contend with as the enemy.

"PLAY BALL."

Eisenhower called a meeting of all of the senior Allied commanders on the Western Front, gathering them together at the fortress of Verdun on the morning of December 19th. Patton, who was involved in heavy fighting near the town of Saarbrücken, realized that the purpose of the meeting would be strategizing a response to the German attack, and he meant to be a step ahead of the other officers in attendance.

Patton ordered his staff officers to come up with three different contingency plans that would get the Third Army out of its current position and start another offensive push. Several different objectives were identified all around the Bulge in the Allied lines that the Germans had created and now occupied. With these plans created and ready in the wings, he went to the meeting with Eisenhower.

❦

The meeting at Verdun was attended by Eisenhower, Patton, Bradley, General Jacob Devers, Major General Kenneth Strong, and Deputy Supreme Commander Air Chief Marshal Arthur Tedder, as well as several staff officers. Eisenhower asked Patton how long it would take him to get six divisions of the Third Army out of their current fighting and into a counterattack to the north in order to relieve the 101st Airborne Division, which had been trapped in the Bulge at Bastogne. Patton answered,

"As soon as you're through with me."

Eisenhower reacted with disbelief, and Patton confirmed that he already had operational orders worked up that would free up three divisions for a full counterattack within 48 hours, on December 21st. Eisenhower, who still believed that it would take more time to mobilize three units, ordered him to commence his counterattack on December 22nd.

❦

Patton immediately left the conference room and phoned his staff officers. He gave them an order that was exactly two words long:

"Play ball."

This was the code phrase that he and his staff had agreed upon, and with those words, his staff began to mobilize three divisions – the 4th Armored Division, the US 80th Infantry Division, and the US 26th Infantry Division. They pulled out of Saarbrücken and struck out northward for Bastogne.

❧

Ultimately, Patton's mobilization involved six entire division stretching from Echternach in Luxembourg, the southern end of the Bulge, all the way to Bastogne on the north. More than 133,000 Third Army vehicles joined an advance that averaged 11 miles per vehicle, followed by support convoys carrying over 62,000 tons of supplies.

❧

On December 21st, Patton and Bradley met to discuss the planned realignment. Patton believed that the Third Army should drive forward toward Koblenz, which would cut off the Bulge and trap all of the Germans who were pressing the assault there. Patton wanted to kill large numbers of Germans, and his plan would have succeeded in that. Bradley, however, wanted to relieve the troops at Bastogne more than he wanted to inflict a bloodbath on their enemy, so he kiboshed the Koblenz attack.

❧

The weather continued to be a factor, and Patton worried that he might have to begin his advance without air support because airplanes could not fly in the storm. He ordered the Third Army's chaplain, Colonel James Hugh O'Neill, to compose a suitable prayer that would entreat the divine to send good weather.

❧

The prayer that O'Neill developed was this:

Almighty and most merciful Father, we humbly beseech Thee, of
Thy great goodness, to restrain these immoderate rains with which
we have had to contend. Grant us fair weather for Battle. Graciously
hearken to us as soldiers who call upon Thee that, armed with Thy
power, we may advance from victory to victory and crush the
oppression and wickedness of our enemies, and establish Thy
justice among men and nations. Amen.

The weather cleared up in time for the offensive, and Patton gave O'Neil a Bronze Star then and there.

The Third Army's 4th Armored Division reached Bastogne on December 26th, opening the way for relief forces and supplies to reach the 101st Airborne, which had suffered greatly during their time in the Bulge. The Battle of the Bulge had inflicted terrible casualties on American forces, who began with a total of 610,000 troops but ended with 502,000. The Battle was the largest and bloodiest battle that Americans would fight in World War II.

Patton was justifiably proud of his accomplishment. He

disengaged six division from one section of front-line combat in the middle of one of the harshest winters on record, then turned it north to relieve pinned down American soldiers. It was his most remarkable achievement.

IX
GERMANY

"A good plan violently executed right now is far better than a perfect plan executed next week."

— GEORGE S. PATTON

By February 1945, the Germans were in a full retreat. They had spent everything they had on their final offensive at the Bulge, rolling the dice and losing. There was nothing left to do but to turn for Germany.

Patton turned for Germany, too.

ON GERMAN SOIL

On February 23, 1945, the US 95th Infantry Division crossed the Saar River and established a bridgehead in the German state of Saarland. Patton used this bridgehead to send units into Saarland, pressing ahead in eagerness to take the battle to the enemy's home. His officers advised against such an immediate crossing of the river, but Patton would not be deterred.

The price for his stubbornness was that the Third Army ran out of the fuel and supplies again. Patton learned that Eisenhower had put him and his men behind the First Army in order of supply, meaning that the First Army would get all of the fuel that they needed while Patton and his men stood in line. This was not acceptable. Ordnance units from the Third Army passed themselves off as being from the First Army and appropriated fuel and supplies from a First Army supply dump.

❧

After this moment of inspired larceny, Patton and his Third Army were on a roll. Between January 29 and March 22, they rolled over the German countryside like a hurricane, taking Trier, Coblenz, Bingen, Worms, Mainz, Kaiserslautern and Ludwigshafen, all cities well within German borders. In the process, they killed or wounded 99,000 German soldiers and took 140,112 Germans soldiers as prisoners of war. This human booty was the entirety of what remained of the German First and Seventh Armies.

❧

During his advance, Patton received orders to bypass Trier, as he didn't have the four divisions that headquarters believed would be needed to take the town. Patton, however, had already taken the town, and he sent a message back to HQ:

> *"Have taken Trier with two divisions. Do you want me to give it back?"*

❧

On March 22, 1945, the Third Army reached the Rhine River, where they built a pontoon bridge. Patton sent a division over that bridge that evening, entering the heart of German territory. He later bragged that he had urinated in the river as he passed over it.

OFLAG XIII-B

❧

In the Langwasser district of Nuremberg, there was a camp called OFLAG XIII-B. It was a prisoner of war camp for American officers captured at the Battle of the Bulge. By the time Patton and his units crossed the Rhine, there were over 1,290 American soldiers imprisoned there.

❧

According to the Red Cross, the conditions were very poor. Each barrack was used to house 200 men. There was no hot water for washing, latrines were few and far between, and the coal that was available for heat during that bitter winter was strictly rationed. All winter, the average interior temperature of the barracks was about 20 degrees Fahrenheit. Food rations were limited, and the men were sick and hungry. One of those men was Lieutenant Colonel John K. Waters – Patton's son-in-law.

On March 26, 1945, Patton decided to liberate the camp. He sent Task Force Baum, which was made up of 314 men, 16 tanks, and assorted other vehicles. The task force was sent 50 miles behind German lines to rescue the suffering American officers.

The raid was an abject failure. There were 32 men killed. Only 35 of the attackers were able to return to the Third Army. All of the vehicles were lost. The rest of the members of Task Force Baum were captured and added to the prison's population, which the Germans evacuated on March 28th. Over 500 American POWs were moved to Nuremberg in the wake of the unsuccessful attack. Eisenhower was furious when he heard about the clandestine action, and Patton admitted that this failed attack was the only mistake he made during the war. He later said that he should have sent a Combat Command instead of a Task Force because a Combat Command would have been three times larger.

HORRIBLE DISCOVERIES

❧

By April, the war was virtually over. The Third Army was largely concerned with managing its contingent of almost 410,000 German prisoners of war. There was little resistance as the army rolled on. On April 14, 1945, Patton was promoted to general, largely in recognition of his accomplishments the year before.

❧

In late April, Patton, Bradley, and Eisenhower saw the horrors of the Nazi regime first hand. They toured the Merkers salt mine, where the Nazis had both slave laborers and an astonishing cache of stolen artwork from all over Europe. As the slaves mined the salt, chambers were created, and the Nazis filled them with stolen plunder. Much was the treasure sacked from the great museums of Europe, but some of it had been taken from the homes of rich Jewish citizens that the regime had murdered.

Patton witnessed the evidence of those murders when he and the other generals toured the Ohrdruf concentration camp. A forced labor and concentration camp, it was part of the Buchenwald complex, and it was the first of the German concentration camps that the Allies saw close up.

The camp was liberated by the Third Army's 4th Armored Division and the 89th Infantry Division on April 4, 1945. When they entered the camp, they found piles of bodies, some of which had been partially cremated on open-air pyres. More bodies were stacked in buildings and covered with lime to hide the smell of decay.

Eisenhower, Patton, and Bradley toured the camp on April 12th, eight days after it had been liberated. The gruesome scene shook all of the generals, and Patton himself was unable to even enter one room where the Germans had stacked the bodies of thirty men who had died of starvation.

Patton described the things he saw in the camp in a lengthy entry in his diary, and his horror was profound. He called the camp

> *"one of the most appalling sights that I have ever seen."*

THE WRAP UP

❧

The Third Army was ordered to go to Bavaria and Czechoslovakia, where Eisenhower believed that the Germans were preparing to make a last stand. This meant that the Red Army would reach Berlin before the Americans, and Patton was appalled by the thought. He believed that the Red Army was a threat to American interests, and it was over protest that he continued on toward Prague.

❧

V-E Day came on May 8th, and Patton's advance was halted. The war was over.

❧

The Third Army had taken Germany from the Rhine to the Elbe. They had captured over 30,000 square miles of German territory, killed 20,000 German soldiers, wounded an additional 47,700, and took over 650,000 Germans, prisoners. Patton lost 2102 men who were killed, 7,954 who were wounded, and 1,591 who were missing.

❧

The Third Army's battle record was the stuff of records. Once they became operational on August 1, 1944, they spent 281 days in continuous combat. They crossed 25 rivers and captured mile upon mile of enemy territory, including some 12,000 cities and towns. In the course of its war, the Third Army killed, wounded or captured over 1.8 million German soldiers, which was six times the number of men in its own roster.

X
AFTER THE FIGHTING

"Yet another war has come to an end, and with it my usefulness to the world."

— GEORGE S. PATTON

Patton desperately wanted to keep fighting even after the war in Europe ended. He requested a transfer to the Pacific Theater of Operations, but this request was ultimately denied. Instead, he was sent to Europe to serve in the occupation forces.

BUT FIRST, AMERICA

Patton returned to the United States for an extended leave in June 1945. He intended to meet his family in Bedford, Massachusetts, but when he arrived, he was greeted by thousands of well-wishers. He went to the Hatch Memorial Shell, a bandstand in Boston, and addressed a crowd of over 20,000, which included 400 wounded veterans of the Third Army. During his address, Patton again stirred up controversy when he inadvertently insulted the Gold Star Mothers in attendance at his speech. He stated that dead soldiers were frequently fools, but that the wounded were heroes. The Gold Star Mothers took these remarks to be a slight against the memories of their fallen sons, and it took some diplomacy to smooth their ruffled feathers.

He spent time in Boston with his family, but later he spoke in both Denver and Los Angeles. At Los Angeles' Memorial

Coliseum, he spoke before a crowd of 100,000. This time, he managed not to offend anyone. He made a brief stop in Washington, D.C., before he went back to Europe.

❧

On June 14, 1945, Patton was named as military governor of Bavaria, where he was to lead the Third Army in its denazification activities.

DEPRESSION AND STRAIN

Patton was in Bavaria when he learned that the war with Japan had ended. He was devastated and convinced that he would never have the opportunity to fight in a war again. He sank into a depression, driven even darker by his dislike for the position of military governor and the task he had been assigned to do. His behavior and his statements became increasingly erratic, and he began to rub his superiors the wrong way.

His niece Jean Gordon returned to his life, seeing him first in London in 1944 and then joining him in Bavaria in 1945. Patton bragged in detail about his sexual conquests and exploits with Jean, but not everyone believed him. Some thought he exaggerated his virility as a response to a fear of growing old and becoming obsolete.

❧

While he was governor of Bavaria, he again garnered criticism. When it was learned that many of the local political posts were still held by members of the Nazi Party, Patton compared them to Democrats and Republicans and stated that these men had probably been compelled to join the party. The media in the United States responded negatively, and Eisenhower was furious.

❧

Eisenhower confronted Patton about his statements. On September 28, 1945, after an extremely heated argument between the two men, Patton was relieved of his position as military governor. On October 7, he was also removed from the leadership of the Third Army. He transferred command to his replacement in a somber and mournful ceremony where he told the assembled soldiers,

> *"All good things must come to an end. The best thing that has ever happened to me thus far is the honor and privilege of having commanded the Third Army."*

❧

Patton was next assigned to command the US 15th Army, which was a generous name given to a small headquarters staff in Bad Nauheim that was dedicated to compiling a history of the war in Europe. He accepted the post because he loved history, but his depression was such that he soon lost interest. Instead, he began to travel, and he saw many different cities on the Continent. He also returned to Stockholm, where he was reunited with other Olympians from the 1912 Games.

❧

When it was time for him to take his Christmas leave, he left for America on December 10th, intending to leave his post with the 15th Army and to never set foot in Europe again.

ACCIDENTAL DEATH

On December 8, 1945, just before his Christmas leave began, Patton was invited to a pheasant hunt outside the German city of Speyer by his chief of staff, Major General Hobart Gay. Gay was hoping that the excursion would lift Patton's flagging spirits. While they were driving, Gay and Patton passed some wrecked cars on the side of the road while they were driving, and Patton commented,

"How awful war is. Think of the waste."

Mere moments later, Patton's car collided at low speed with an American army truck. Gay and other passengers received only minor bumps and bruises, but Patton hit his head against the glass that separated the front and back seats. He suffered a gash in his head, which bled copiously, and he complained of feeling paralyzed and having difficulty breathing.

❧

His companions took him to a hospital in Heidelberg, where he was diagnosed with a compression fracture and dislocation of the third and fourth cervical vertebrae. His broken neck and the subsequent spinal cord injury rendered him paralyzed from the neck down.

❧

He spent the next 12 days in traction while doctors attempted to relieve the pressure on his spinal cord. Patton's wife flew in from America, and she was the only non-medical visitor who was allowed to see him. Patton was told that he would never again ride a horse or even have a normal life, at which point he commented,

"This is a hell of a way to die."

❧

George S. Patton died in his sleep on December 21, 1945. The cause of death was pulmonary edema and congestive heart failure. He was buried with wartime casualties of the Third Army in the Luxembourg American Cemetery.

XI
LEGACY

"It is foolish and wrong to mourn the men who died. Rather we should thank God that such men lived."

— GEORGE S. PATTON

Patton's life was a patchwork of a hard-driving leadership style, a colorful and sarcastic personality, and a series of dire political missteps. His image is often contradictory. On one hand, he was a hot spark who could often fly off the handle and say and do things that were injurious to himself and others. On the other hand, he was a gifted orator whose capacity to inspire his troops was second to none. Reconciling those elements of his being can sometimes be a tricky proposition.

SINGULAR STYLE

Patton intentionally created a larger-than-life image for himself in the hopes that his troops would find it inspiring. He always carried two ivory-gripped pistols, one on each hip, and when he appeared in public, he was often wearing a well-polished helmet and riding pants and boots. He purposefully held his face in a dour and almost angry expression that he called his "***war face***."

He would command and direct training exercises from a tank that was painted red, white and blue. His jeep had to be a stand-out, as well – it had oversized rank placards and a klaxon-style horn that he used to announce his approach from a distance. To Patton, leadership was more than just commanding a body of men; it was all about making an impact and becoming a symbol.

Unlike the unassuming Eisenhower and the other men of the officer corps, all of whom tried to blend in with their troops on the battlefield, Patton tried to stand out. He wore his rank insignia during battles, and once he even rode into a German-held village on the top of his tank, intending to inspire courage in his men.

He was a favorite with the troops, more approachable and charismatic than most of the generals of his day. He was casually profane, cursing often in his speech, which his men adored, and which consistently irritated and offended other generals, especially Omar Bradley. He was blunt, witty, sarcastic and resolutely dedicated to speaking without thinking.

Patton could also be an extremely hard taskmaster. He would ruthlessly correct and then ridicule subordinates for infractions both real and perceived, but at the same time, he was quick to praise them when they did well. He had no tolerance for failure in himself or others, but he only fired one general during the Second World War, unlike Bradley, who fired several. He was known for the care he took for his enlisted soldiers, and he often personally saw to it that they had things like blankets and extra socks, two things that were frequently in short supply on the front.

On subjects of race, he was often bigoted, probably as a result of his roots in the American South and his family history of fighting for the Confederacy. He stated that he didn't believe African-Americans were capable of thinking quickly enough to be effective in a tank, but he also made more strides than any other officer in integrating the troops under his command.

❧

His spiritual views were also unorthodox. He read and respected the Koran, but he believed that the "***fatalistic teachings of Mohammad***" were the reason for the "***arrested development of the Arab***." He was frequently anti-Semitic in his speech. He was nominally Christian, but he believed firmly in reincarnation, and it was his personal conviction that he had lived before as a Roman legionary and had possibly died in a past life while fighting for Napoleon.

❧

Patton was, without doubt, one of the greatest armored warfare commanders that the American military has ever produced. Even today, tank crews are trained in accordance with the aggressive plans that Patton developed for his men. The first American tank to be designed after the Second World War was christened the M46 Patton, something that he would have enjoyed.

❧

Patton has come down to us today as something of a folk hero. His colorful nature, the portrayals of him in film and television, and the many stories about his life and career have made him a towering figure in the history of the American military.

YOUR FREE EBOOK!

As a way of saying thank you for reading our book, we're offering you a free copy of the below eBook.

Happy Reading!

GO WWW.THEHISTORYHOUR.COM/CLEO/

Made in the USA
Monee, IL
21 December 2020

55087410R00062